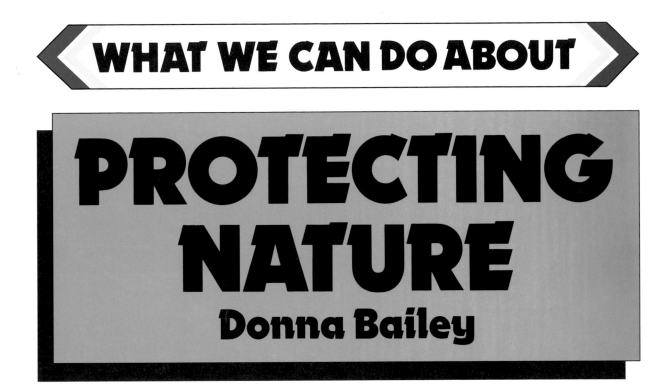

WHAT WE CAN DO ABOUT

PROTECTING NATURE

Donna Bailey

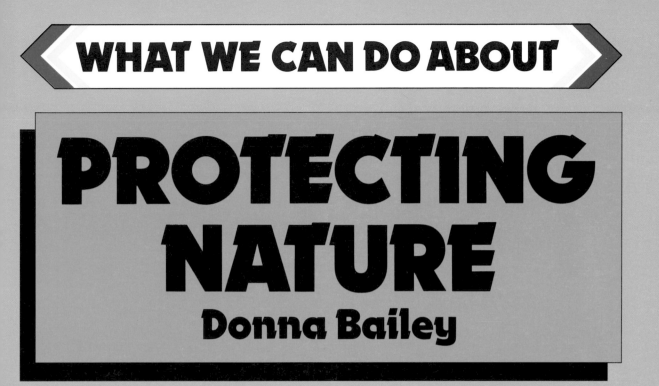

WHAT WE CAN DO ABOUT

PROTECTING NATURE

Donna Bailey

Franklin Watts

New York   London   Toronto   Sydney

Franklin Watts
387 Park Avenue South
New York, NY 10016

Design: Julian Holland Publishing Ltd.
Illustrator: Martin Smillie
Picture Research: Alison Renwick
Printed in Italy

Library of Congress Cataloging-in-Publication Data
Bailey, Donna.
    Protecting nature/by Donna Bailey.
        p.   cm. — (What we can do about)
    Includes index.
    Summary: Focuses on dangers posed to nature and ways of protecting nature.
    ISBN 0-531-11080-X
    1. Nature conservation — Juvenile literature. 2. Environmental protection —
Juvenile literature. [1. Nature conservation. 2. Environmental
protection.] I. Title. II. Series: Bailey, Donna. What we can do about.
QH75.B35   1992
363.7'0525 — dc20   91-11534
                                                    CIP
                                                      AC

Photograph acknowledgments
t = top *b* = bottom
Cover: Dr Norman Myers/Bruce Coleman Ltd.
p6 C Jones/The Environmental Picture Library, 7 Hans Reinhard/Bruce Coleman
Ltd, 8*t* Paul Glendell/The Environmental Picture Library, 8*b* George McCarthy/
Bruce Coleman Ltd, 9 Stephen Dalton/NHPA, 10 WWF/Timm Rautert/Bruce
Coleman Ltd, 11 Stephen Krasemann/NHPA, 12 Christer Andreason/Robert
Harding Picture Library, 13*t* N A Callow/NHPA, 13*b* Anthony Bannister/NHPA,
14 Jane Burton/Bruce Coleman Ltd, 15*t* Kim Taylor/Bruce Coleman Ltd, 15*b* Holt
Studios, 16*t* Robert Brook/The Environmental Picture Library, 16*b* David
Woodfall/NHPA, 17 Chris Fairclough Colour Library, 18 Midgley/Greenpeace, 19*t*
Uwe Walz/Bruce Coleman Ltd, 19*b* Gerald Cubitt/Bruce Coleman Ltd, 21 David
Meredith/Bruce Coleman Ltd, 22 Christian Zuber/Bruce Coleman Ltd, 24*t* H
Girardet/The Environmental Picture Library, 24*b* Chris Fairclough Colour Library,
25 Mark N Boulton/Bruce Coleman Ltd, 26 Hans Reinhard/Bruce Coleman Ltd, 27
Chris Fairclough Colour Library.

Contents

Before it's too late

When a type of animal or plant no longer appears in the wild, we say it is **extinct**. Throughout the world, over 6,000 **species** of animals and 25,000 species of plants are now in danger of becoming extinct. We must all make greater efforts to save them. Protecting nature means making sure that wild plants and animals, such as these gorillas, are not harmed by **pollution** or disturbed in the places where they live.

There are ways in which you can help to protect nature. When you are walking in the countryside, leave the wildflowers for someone else to enjoy. Species like snowdrops and the orchids in our picture were once often seen growing in the wild, but orchids especially have become very rare because people have picked them or pulled them up.

Never leave litter, for it can harm animals. Plastic bottles, bags and nets can trap tiny creatures, and broken glass can cut animals' paws.

To protect plants and animals, we must protect the places where they live, their **habitats**.

A wood is the habitat for birds who build their nests in the trees and look for insects living under the bark. Some plants can only grow in the shade under the trees. So, if the wood is cleared, it is not just that the trees are destroyed. Also, the plants, insects, animals and birds that live there lose their homes.

For many animals, it is important that their habitat be linked to other similar habitats by a narrow strip, or corridor. Bushes can provide a corridor between separate patches of woodland. Field mice and other small animals can travel through the bushes from one wood to another. They need not go into the open where they would be in danger of being caught by larger animals.

Fussy feeders

Some animals feed on only one species of plant. If that plant becomes extinct, the animals will die out, too. Giant pandas feed only on bamboo. When the Chinese set up panda wildlife parks in their country, they made sure that these parks were linked by bamboo corridors, so that the groups of pandas could mix. By protecting the panda, the Chinese hope that the numbers of these animals will increase. Only about 600 pandas live in the wild today.

The tiny silver nesodyne fly is found only among the fleshy leaves of the silversword plant. The plant grows only on the sides of the dry volcanic craters on the island of Hawaii. The silversword plant takes 20 years to store enough water to produce a flower head 2 m (6.5 ft) high, which lasts for 3 weeks. Then the whole plant dies. Such a plant has only one chance to produce seeds and new plants. Silversword plants are eaten by goats, which were taken to the island by **settlers**. Both the plants and the nesodyne fly are in great danger of becoming extinct.

All plants and animals depend on each other. To destroy one species of plant may also mean that we have destroyed the habitat of the insects and animals that feed on it.

Nature in the garden

Gardens are unlikely to contain many rare species of wildlife, but they can provide valuable habitats for wild plants and animals. Even if your family does not have a garden, you could grow a few plants in pots on a balcony or in a window box. If you choose suitable plants, like asters and heather, they will attract insects such as butterflies and moths.

In a larger garden you and your parents could grow some wildflowers to help preserve wild species. Do not dig up wildflowers from the countryside, but plant seeds that have been specially bred for wildflower gardens. A bed of wildflowers can be just as colorful as a rose bed.

In your garden try to grow a wide variety of plants and shrubs and include some of the species that are known to attract insects. For example, the flowers of a buddleia bush attract butterflies, and nasturtiums and convolvulus attract hoverflies like the one in the photograph.

Some insects, including dragonflies, eat other insects and so help control garden pests. Aphids are small insects that suck sap from plant stems. This weakens the plants and stops them from growing properly. Aphids are eaten by the young (larvae) of dragonflies and lacewings, and by ladybugs, as shown in the photograph.

Spiders also eat insect pests. They spin a new web every morning. Then they hide nearby until an insect gets trapped in the sticky strands of the web.

Frogs and toads in the garden eat slugs, wood lice and other insects.

Natural pest control

Small **mammals** like shrews and moles can be useful in the garden. They eat large numbers of garden pests such as wood lice, millipedes, wireworms and slugs. Ask your parents to leave a pile of logs and autumn leaves in a quiet corner of the garden. If you are lucky, one of these small creatures may choose to spend the winter in this pile.

Many species of birds feed on slugs, aphids and other pests. Bird feeders and nest boxes help attract birds to your garden. It makes sense to encourage helpful wildlife into the garden so that they can control the pests. This is better than using chemical **insecticides** and other **pesticides** which may kill the pests but also harm bees, butterflies and moths.

Some people believe that certain plants can protect others from pests. This mixing of particular plants is called companion planting. People say that the smell of herbs like sage and thyme stops slugs from eating tender, young leaves. Also if lavender is planted near roses it helps protect them against aphids.

Onions planted next to carrots are said to deter carrot flies. The maggots of the carrot fly burrow into the roots of the carrots and make young plants die and older carrots rot, like the one in the photograph. Why not persuade your parents to try out some of these ideas on companion planting in the vegetable garden?

15

If your school does not have a special wildlife area, perhaps you could persuade your teacher to help you set one up. Even a small space, such as a narrow strip of land between the playground and a fence, can be valuable to local wildlife if it is taken care of properly. If more land is available you could make a wild flower meadow, a **tree nursery,** or a pond.

Conservation groups have people working for them who will be able to tell you and your teachers how to set up and take care of a school wildlife area. These groups may also own or look after other wildlife sites. Why not offer to help with some of the work on these sites?

In many countries children help clear out overgrown ponds and streams. They help in counts and surveys of birds and animals. The information they gather helps people to find out what species are under threat of extinction.

Conservation groups often organize talks about nature and visits to local sites. If you learn as much as you can about nature, you will know how to help protect it.

When you visit these sites try to disturb the wildlife as little as possible. Take notes of the different species of bird you see at different times of the year. You could also make drawings of the flowers and wildlife, so that you can identify them later. Build up a record of local wildlife in a notebook. Perhaps you could create a wildlife database on a computer in class with some of your friends.

Threats to nature

As the number of people in the world continues to grow, it is important to think about the effect our way of life has on nature. More houses are needed for the world's growing population. Today, we expect a better standard of living than in the past. In many countries, each family expects to own at least one car as well as household appliances, such as televisions and a washing machine. Factories are needed to make all these goods, while cars need roads to travel on. New houses, factories and roads take up land that was once the home of wild animals and plants.

Sometimes wildlife sites are flooded to make large lakes, which provide water for people and crops. Or wet, marshy land is drained for farmland. The marshland is often a feeding place for water birds, like those in our picture. Naturally planted areas have been uprooted to make bigger fields which can be farmed more easily. Meadows full of wildflowers have been replaced by fields of food crops.

Nature can be harmed by pollution, which makes places dirty and unsuitable for animal and plant life. Sticky, black oil spilled in the sea covers birds and other sea creatures. Many die because they cannot remove the oil from their feathers, or they eat food that contains the oil. The penguins in the picture are lucky. Oil from a spill is being cleaned from their feathers.

Polluted water from factories and farms is sometimes allowed to flow into rivers and streams. Gradually the water creatures and plants are poisoned by the pollution and they die.

Nature on the farm

Many farmers spray chemicals called **herbicides** and pesticides on their crops to help prevent weeds and to kill insects and other pests. Farmers also use chemical fertilizers to make the crops grow better. All these chemicals harm wildlife.

The pesticide spray may drift over from the field being treated to nearby fields and woods. It then gets onto the food eaten by wildlife and harms species other than the pests. Some pesticides can become **concentrated** and more harmful as one animal eats another in a **food chain**.

A food chain

the sun's energy makes plants grow

pesticide is sprayed on fields

mice and rabbits are eaten by owls

mice and rabbits are eaten by foxes

corn and grass are eaten by mice and rabbits

One way to discourage the use of pesticides and fertilizers on crops is to buy **organically** grown food. Organic farmers try to work with nature. Instead of chemical fertilizers, they use **compost** made from decayed plant material or animal waste. They spray muck or compost over the fields to make the grass grow better.

Studies in Denmark have found that there are more birds on organic farms than on those using chemicals. When a farmer in Britain stopped spraying herbicide on a strip of land around the edge of his fields, the number of some species of birds tripled within a year, and the number of butterfly species increased from 4 to 21.

Goods from far away

You can help people in other countries protect their local wildlife by being careful about what goods you buy. It is now **illegal** to sell goods made from animals in danger of becoming extinct: for example, ivory objects made from the tusks of elephants. But if people still try to buy ivory, other people will continue to kill the elephants.

Sometimes, animals are taken from their habitats to be sold as pets. Many animals die during the journey from the place of their capture to the place where they will be sold. Unusual pets, such as parrots, are far better left in the wild where they can enjoy their natural life.

Many of our indoor potted plants grow in the wild in warmer climates. Some potted plants are specially bred for sale, but others are uprooted from their natural habitats. As a result, some of these plants are no longer found in the places where they used to grow. Scientists believe that only three species of the world's most popular houseplant, the African violet, are still growing wild in tropical forests.

Saving the rainforests

Tropical rainforests are a habitat that is in particular danger. Over 20 hectares (50 acres) are destroyed every minute. We must try to save the rainforests, because they are very important in the control of the world's climate. They are also home to many unusual plants and animals. The forests give us food and medicines. All the goods in the picture came from plants or trees that once grew in the rainforests.

Zoos and botanic gardens

Most of us will only ever see some of the world's rarest animals and plants in zoos, wildlife parks and **botanic gardens**. In the past, zoos and gardens collected rare species from the wild. Many died because they were not kept in suitable conditions. Today, most zoos get their animals by breeding them. Some breeding programs have been so successful that species have been reintroduced into the wild. By 1962, the Arabian oryx was in danger of becoming extinct. Three oryx were taken from the wild and a careful breeding program started. By 1983, their numbers had increased enough for some of the oryx to be released back into the wild.

Activities

1 Choose a plant or animal that is in danger of extinction, for example, the golden lion tamarin, the snow leopard, the thick-billed parrot in the United States or the black rhino. Where does it live and why is it under threat? How many are left and are there any projects or laws that are helping to protect it? You could write an article about your endangered animal and add a drawing or photograph of it.

If you and your friends choose different species, you could make a newspaper, book, or a display, for other children in your school to read.
2 Try to identify the birds that visit your garden or school grounds. Check which birds prefer what type of food, and if you have a bird feeder, you could leave food out for them. Leave food out regularly because the birds will depend on the feeder as a source of food.

3 In the autumn, look under the trees and collect some fallen seeds. Take a fallen leaf as well to help you identify the tree. Then you could plant the seeds in pots filled with moist earth mixed with a little compost. Do not forget to label each pot! Check beforehand that your seeds don't need any special treatment first. Some types of tree seeds need to be frozen or scraped with sandpaper before they will grow.

Keep the soil moist, and plant out the seedlings in a tree nursery when they are big enough.

Glossary

botanic garden: a garden often open to the public, where rare or special plants are grown.

compost: material added to the soil to make it more fertile.

concentrate: to increase the strength of something by adding more of it into the same space.

conservation group: an organization that aims to take care of, or conserve, nature.

extinct: disappeared, no longer living.

food chain: a series of living things that depend on each other for food. A plant is eaten by an animal, which in turn is eaten by another animal.

habitat: the place where a plant or animal makes its home.

herbicide: a chemical sprayed onto crops that kills weeds.

illegal: against the law.

insecticide: a chemical sprayed onto crops that kills insects.

mammal: an animal that gives birth to live young that feed on their mother's milk.

organic: describes food that is grown without using chemical fertilizers or pesticides.

pesticide: a chemical used to kill insects.

pollution: something that dirties or poisons the air, land or water.

settlers: people who make their home in a new country.

species: a single group of identical animals or plants that can breed to produce like offspring.

tree nursery: a patch of ground where small trees are grown until they are big enough to be planted out.

tropical rainforest: a hot, damp forest with an annual rainfall of at least 254 cm (100 in) found in the regions close to the Equator.

Index